KINGS
50.. ...-y mill Road
Atlanta, Georgia 30338

Some Basics About
WOMEN'S GYMNASTICS
By Ed and Ruth Radlauer

Gemini Series

AN ELK GROVE BOOK
ℚ CHILDRENS PRESS, CHICAGO

Created for CHILDRENS PRESS
by Radlauer Productions, Incorporated

With special thanks to Sina Lock, Carol Mona, and Claire Takaki of the YMCA East Whittier Family Branch, as well as to Carol Sandhu of Idyllwild, California.

Artwork page 18, Cathy Pavia
Photo credits:
Front cover, page 12, 30 by Rich Kenney,
courtesy of International GYMNAST magazine.

Library of Congress Cataloging in Publication Data
Radlauer, Edward.
   Some basics about women's gymnastics.
   (Gemini series)
   "An Elk Grove book."
   SUMMARY: A brief introduction to the history, equipment, and basic movements and techniques of women's gymnastics.
   1. Gymnastics for women—Juvenile literature.
[1. Gymnastics for women] I. Radlauer, Ruth Shaw, joint author. II. Title.
GV464.R26   1980   796.4'1   79-21826
ISBN 0-516-07687-6

Copyright © by Regensteiner Publishing Enterprises, Inc.
All rights reserved. Published simultaneously in Canada.
Printed in the United States of America.

3 4 5 6 7 8 9 10 11 12 13 14 15 R 86 85 84 83 82 81

Contents

	page
To Paint a Picture	4
Gymnastics Yesterday	6
Gymnastics Today	8
The Balance Beam	10
More Beam	12
Floor Exercises	14
The Vault	16
The Half On, Half Off	18
The Uneven Parallel Bars	20
More Parallel Bars	22
A Coach	24
Equipment	26
Where Does it Hurt?	28
Competition	30
Index	32

To Paint a Picture

Some people use brushes to paint pictures. But you can paint beautiful pictures with your body if you become a gymnast.

Here's how.

In women's gymnastics you use muscles, skill, strength, and body control to create beautiful pictures.

Gymnastics can be moving or still pictures. Your routine starts with a still. Then it becomes a movie as you run, leap, turn, even fly. And the routine ends with a controlled, very still pose.

In a floor exercise, you paint many moods as you move around the large floor mat. On uneven parallel bars you paint whirling circles and points. The vault helps your pictures take off and fly. In a narrow space on the beam, your painting flows quietly with control and grace.

Does that sound interesting? Let's see where it all started.

Gymnastics Yesterday

If yesterday means hundreds of years ago, gymnastics was mostly for men. What kind of men?

The men were soldiers, getting ready for war, as usual. The soldiers rode horses and they wanted to be able to get on and off fast.

   For practice the soldiers used make-believe horses. The make-believe horse had a long thin body, four legs, a fake head and a fake tail. To train, a soldier ran up to the horse, jumped on, waved a spear, and jumped off. Later, people gave up the spear. But gymnasts still use the make-believe horse.

   If yesterday means thousands of years ago, people went into gymnastics for better health, to cure sickness, and to develop their bodies. Some gymnastic events had prizes for boxing and wrestling games.

   Then in the early 1880s, Dr. Frederick Jahn designed some new equipment. That led to—

Gymnastics Today

Both men and women become gymnasts now. Women's events are the balance beam, vault (horse), uneven parallel bars, and floor exercise.

What does it take to become a gymnast today?

You need strong muscles and a firm body. You need to take care of your body by exercising and careful eating.

To win at gymnastics, you need to spend many hours in training. In fact, training may take up most of your time.

A gymnast must concentrate, think hard. You need to control and discipline yourself to work, even when you'd rather do something else. Most of all you need courage to be a gymnast. You must have courage to try new movements that challenge your growing skill.

Do you have discipline and courage? Can you concentrate? Can you keep at it, even when mistakes make you feel like quitting? Yes? Then you just may be a gymnast.

The Balance Beam

It's four inches (10.16cm) wide and 16 feet (4.87m) long. It may sit on the floor or be four feet (1.21m) off the ground. This equipment takes balance. It's the beam.

Your job, your first gymnastic exercise, is to walk the beam from end to end. Sounds easy—until you try it. Then you wish you had balance like the cat on the backyard fence.

You need balance because this is the balance beam. So you walk, wobble, lean, twist—and fall off. But that's all right. You're a beginner, just learning to balance.

Soon there's more than walking. You begin to place your feet with control. Your body is steady, your steps straight. You hold out your arms, fingers straight. Even your face says you feel balanced on the beam.

More Beam

Now you know how to walk, stop, turn, and balance. It's time to try more difficult stunts on this narrow piece of equipment.

How about a walkover? Start from a bend and go forward into a handstand with one foot down, one foot up. Now go all the way over, up into a standing position. You may also try a back walkover. Just like a front walkover, only backwards.

Gymnasts also do leaps on the beam. Leap high, legs out straight, and land. Your landing must be very steady, as still as a statue, a graceful statue.

Yes, on the beam, or when using any other equipment, the more graceful you look, the more points you'll have when you finish the routine.

Floor Exercises

You do them on the floor. So it must be easy. But is it? After all, it's just you, the floor, and the music.

Music? Is there dancing? Yes, almost. It's dancing and tumbling. Good gymnasts take dancing lessons, then mix dance with their tumbling skills for floor exercises. Dance lessons teach you to move with style as you express yourself and your feelings.

Floor exercises are done on a 40 by 40 foot (12.2m.) mat. Besides dance and ballet movements, gymnasts do leaps, twirls, flips, and handsprings.

Your routine is timed. During the time you must do different movements to the different kinds of music. You must cover most of the 40 by 40 foot (12.2m) mat. If your routine fits the mood of the music you select, you'll be doing good floor exercises worth lots of points in competition.

The Vault

Gymnasts used to call it the horse. Now it's the vault. And it's time for you to vault over the horse. How does that work?

At first you don't do it alone. You need help from people called spotters. Spotters help you make your vault and keep from crashing.

For the vault you must first learn the correct run or approach. The approach includes your jump from the spring or reuther board. After you learn to make correct approaches, you're ready for your first vault stunt, the squat.

To do the squat, run, jump, and tuck your legs under. Use your hands to help as you go over the vault.

After the squat, you can try the straddle. Legs apart and hands between your legs as you go over. The straddle is a little harder than the squat.

As you get more skill on the vault, you may be ready for—

The Half On, Half Off

Does that mean you jump half way onto and half way off the vault? It may sound like that, but it's really a very difficult vault routine with flying half turns.

Here's how you do the half on, half off.

Your running approach needs just the right speed and step so you can

1. Make a balanced and controlled head-over-heels leap from the spring board.

2. Include a flying half turn of the body in your vault.

3. Use your arms and hands for a strong push off from the vault into another flying half turn.

4. Land as steady as a statue with your back to the horse.

This stunt requires two flying half turns. No wonder people say the half on, half off is a very difficult gymnastic routine.

The Uneven Parallel Bars

In women's gymnastics there are two bars, one higher than the other. Under the bars is a mat for a dismount. The mat makes dismounts softer, especially if you happen to make a sudden landing.

To start, you jump, grab the bar, and hang. Simple enough. But after a few tries your arms and shoulders start to hurt. Your hands stick to the bar. Chalk powder helps your hands, but before long you have blisters.

Blisters or not, you go for the higher bar. You hang, swing to the lower bar, then dismount. You've done your first trick on the bars.

Later, you're ready for the kip. In a kip, you grab the low bar, swing, bend your legs at the hips, and swing up over the bar. From the kip you're ready for more difficult bar routines. Your hands are ready, too. They're getting hard callouses. Callouses are the sign of a hard working gymnast.

More Parallel Bars

After you know how to hang, jump, and kip, you can fly from bar to bar. You're ready to learn more difficult tricks or stunts.

You may try a flight from the lower bar to the higher bar and hang with your body forming a letter V.

Other stunts include doing airborne turns as you fly between bars. Or you may do turns as you dismount.

Another stunt gymnasts like is moving the body in a circle around the bars with a balanced stop at the top of the circle. Your stop won't be long, but it should be steady.

These stunts are all hard when you first try them. But with practice, most gymnastic tricks get easier. Never easy, just easier. To make your routines better and easier, you need—

A Coach

In gymnastics, as in other sports, a good coach is important. How do you pick a coach? How can you tell which coach will make you a winner?

You can't. You might try your winning friend's coach because you want to be a winner, too. After a while you find you don't get along with that coach. It's hard to say why. But you have learned an important gymnastics lesson. Don't choose a coach just to make you a winner. To pick a coach, ask these questions.

1. Do I trust and believe in this person?
2. Will this coach help me be a good winner as well as a good loser?
3. Will the coach cut down on injuries with good spotting?
4. Does this coach know gymnastics and keep the team excited and interested?

If you and your coach work well together, you may both become winners in gymnastics.

Equipment

In women's gymnastics there are two kinds of equipment: the kind you buy and the kind someone else buys.

You buy just a few things. These are leotards, sockies, and a warmup suit. Leotards cling to your body and don't get in the way as you do gymnastics. Sockies cover your feet, and you need a warmup suit before and after your workouts. For comfort and a neat look, you need something to hold your hair, especially if it's long.

The equipment you won't buy includes the horse, bars, balance beam, chalk, and mats. But in a way you do buy these when you pay for lessons. In fact, you may spend the most money on membership in a club, if that's where you train.

If you get to be very good, you may need clothes and a suitcase for travel to events in faraway places. Let's hope you need a special place to show all your trophies.

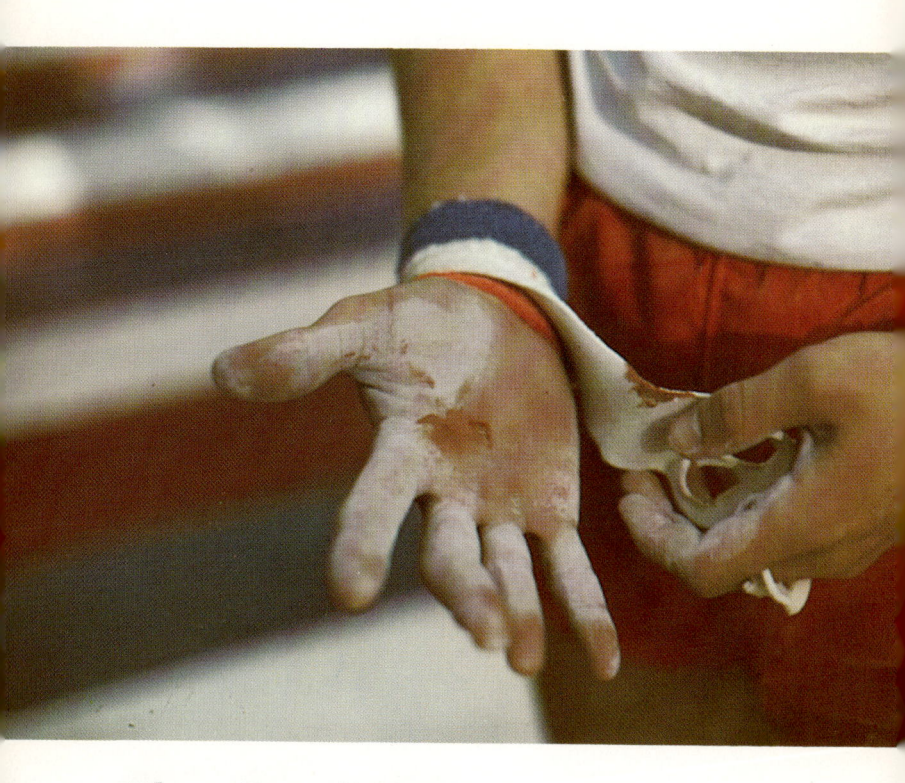

Where Does it Hurt?

Sometimes it hurts all over. You may get some extra hurts when you try a new stunt. If a muscle gets sore, you may need tapes or bandages.

With the help of tapes and bandages, you may be able to carry on your exercises.

If you get a bad strain, or sprain, stop. Get some ice. Packing a strain or sprain in ice keeps it from swelling and getting painful. Ice packs and careful exercise will help you get back to your routines.

Blisters can be painful. But some coaches teach you to go right on, pain or not. You never know when you might have to get along with the pain of a blister or rip during competition.

A shin splint is serious because a muscle has pulled away from your shin bone. If you get a shin splint, you may be out of training for about six weeks. But if you take care of your hurts, you'll be ready to go on to—

Competition

You start small. You compete with gymnasts from other clubs. If you work hard, you may go on to state competitions, even national ones. Some hope to make it to the Olympics, the big international competition held every four years.

To get to the Olympics, you work for years. You win. You lose. You try. You wait. You give most of your time to practice. Your family spends a lot of money on training and coaches.

Finally, one day, Olympic judges are scoring your routines. For most events you start with 10 points on each routine. Judges take points off for faults, mistakes, falls, or wobbles. If your points add up to the highest score in your class, you get a gold medal. The second-place gymnast gets silver; third gets bronze.

But whether you aim for the Olympics or not, you can enjoy the work, the friends, and a body that feels great. In gymnastics you'll enjoy using your body to paint beautiful pictures.

Index

approach, 17, 19

balance, 10, 11, 12, 19
ballet, 15
beam, 5, 8, 10, 11, 12, 13, 27
blisters, 21, 29
boxing, 7

callouses, 21
chalk powder, 21, 27
club, 27, 30
coach, 24, 25, 29, 31
competition, 15, 29, 30
courage, 9

dancing, 15
discipline, 9
dismount, 20, 21, 23

equipment, 7, 10, 12, 13, 26, 27
exercising, 9, 11, 29

faults, 31
floor exercise, 5, 8, 14, 15
half on, half off, 18, 19

handsprings, 15
handstand, 13
health, 7
horse, 7, 8, 16, 19, 27

injuries, 25

Jahn, Dr. Frederick, 7
judges, 31

kip, 21, 23

leotards, 27

mat, floor exercises, 5, 15, 27
mat, under bars, 20, 27
medal, 31
men, 6, 7, 8
muscles, 5, 9, 28, 29
music, 14, 15

Olympics, 30, 31

points, 13, 15, 31

reuther board, 17
rip, 29
routine, 5, 13, 15, 17, 18, 19, 21, 23, 29, 31

scoring, 31
shin splint, 29
sockies, 27
soldiers, 7
spotter, 17
spotting, 25
sprain, strain, 29
spring board, 17, 19
squat, 17
straddle, 17

training, 9, 27, 29, 31
trophies, 27
tumbling, 15

uneven parallel bars, 5, 8, 20, 21, 22, 23, 27

vault, 5, 8, 16, 17, 18, 19

walkover, 11, 13
warmup suit, 27
wrestling, 7

32